THE CHALDÆAN

ORACLES OF ZOROASTER

THE CHALDÆAN

ORACLES OF ZOROASTER

By Sapere Aude. (W.Wynn Westcott)

Redited and revised by Octavia & Co. Press
For The Modern Ancient Reader.

PREFACE

By Sapere Aude.

These oracles are considered to embody many of the principal features of Chaldæan philosophy. They have come down to us through Greek translations and were held in the greatest esteem throughout antiquity, a sentiment which was shared alike by the early Christian Fathers and the later Platonists. The doctrines contained therein are attributed to Zoroaster, though to which particular Zoroaster is not known; historians give notices of as many as six different individuals all bearing that name, which was probably the title of the Prince of the Magi, and a generic term. The word Zoroaster is by various authorities differently derived: Kircher furnishes one of the most interesting derivations when he seeks to show that it comes from TzURA : a figure, and TzIUR : to fashion, Ash : fire, and STR : hidden; from these he gets the words Zairaster : fashioning images of hidden fire; or Tzuraster : the image of secret things. Others derive it from Chaldee and Greek words meaning "a contemplator of the Stars."

It is not, of course, pretended that this collection as it stands is other than disjointed and fragmentary, and it is more than probable that the true sense of many passages has been obscured, and even in some cases hopelessly obliterated, by inadequate translation. Where it has been possible to do so, an attempt has been made to elucidate doubtful or ambiguous expressions, either by modifying the existing translation from the Greek, where deemed permissible, or by appending annotations.

It has been suggested by some that these Oracles are of Greek invention, but it has already been pointed out by Stanley that Picus de Mirandula (Giovanni Pico della Mirandula) assured Ficinus (Marcilio Ficino) that he had the Chaldee Original in his possession, in which those things which are faulty and defective in the Greek are read perfect and entire," and Ficinus indeed states that he found this manuscript upon the death of Mirandula. In addition to this, it should be noted that here and there in the original Greek version, words occur which are not of Greek extraction at all, but are Hellenised Chaldee.

Berosus is said to be the first who introduced the writings of the Chaldæans concerning Astronomy and Philosophy among the Greeks, and it is certain that the traditions of Chaldea very largely influenced Greek thought. Taylor considers that some of these mystical utterances are the sources whence the sublime conceptions of Plato were formed, and large commentaries were written upon them by Porphyry, Iamblichus, Proclus, Pletho and Psellus. That men of such great learning and sagacity should have thought so highly of these Oracles, is a fact which in itself should commend them to our attention.

The term "Oracles" was probably bestowed upon these epigrammatic utterances in order to enforce the idea of their profound and deeply mysterious nature. The Chaldæans, however, had an Oracle, which they venerated as highly as the Greeks did that at Delphi.

We are indebted to both Psellus and Pletho, for comments at some length upon the Chaldæan Oracles, and the collection adduced by these writers has been considerably enlarged by Franciscus Patricius, who made many additions from Proclus, Hermias, Simplicius, Damascius, Synesius, Olympiodorus,

Nicephorus and Arnobius; his collection, which comprised some 324 oracles under general heads, was published in Latin in 1593, and constitutes the groundwork of the later classification arrived at by Taylor and Cory; all of these editions have been utilized in producing the present revise.

A certain portion of these Oracles collected by Psellus, appear to be correctly attributed to a Chaldæan Zoroaster of very early date, and are marked **Z**," following the method indicated by Taylor, with one or two exceptions. Another portion is attributed to a sect of philosophers named Theurgists, who flourished during the reign of Marcus Antoninus, upon the authority of Proclus, and these are marked "**T**." Oracles additional to these two series and of less definite source are marked "**Z** or **T**." Other oracular passages from miscellaneous authors are indicated by their names.

THE ORACLES OF ZOROASTER.

CAUSE. GOD.
FATHER. MIND. FIRE.
MONAD. DYAD. TRIAD.

1. God is. He, having the head of the Hawk, is the first. He is incorruptible, eternal, unbegotten, indivisible, dissimilar; the dispenser of all good; indestructible; the best of the good, the Wisest of the wise. He is the Father of Equity and Justice; self-taught, physical, perfect, and wise. It is he who inspires the Sacred Philosophy.

2. Theurgists assert that He is a God and celebrate him as both older and younger, as a circulating and eternal God, as understanding the whole number of all things moving in the World, and moreover infinite through his power and energizing a spiral force.

3. The God of the Universe, eternal, limitless, both young and old, having a spiral force.

4. The Eternal Æon -- according to the Oracle -- is the cause of never failing life, of unwearied power and unsluggish energy.

5. Hence the inscrutable God is called silent by the divine ones; is said to consent with Mind, and to be known to human souls through the power of the Mind alone.

6. The Chaldæans call the God Dionysus (or Bacchus), Iao in the Phoenician tongue (instead of the Intelligible Light), and he is also called Sabaoth, signifying that he is above the Seven poles, that is the Demiurges.

7. Containing all things in the one summit of his own Hyparxis, He Himself subsists wholly beyond.

8. Measuring and bounding all things.

9. For nothing imperfect emanates from the Paternal Principle,

10. The Father effused not Fear, but He infused persuasion.

11. The Father has apprehended Himself, and has not restricted his Fire to his own intellectual power.

12. Such is the Mind which is energized before energy, while yet it had not gone forth, but abode in the Paternal Depth, and in the Adytum of God nourished silence.

13. All things have issued from that one Fire. The Father perfected all things, and delivered them over to the Second Mind, whom all Nations of Men call the First.

14. The Second Mind conducts the Empyrean World.

15. What the Intelligible says, it says by understanding.

16. Power is with them, but Mind is from Him.

17. The Mind of the Father rides on the subtle Guiders, which glitter with the tracings of inflexible and relentless Fire.
18. After the Paternal Conception I the Soul reside, a heat animating all things ... For he placed The Intelligible in the Soul, and the Soul in dull body, even so the Father of Gods and Men placed them in us.

19. Natural works co-exist with the intellectual light of the Father. It is the Soul which adorned the vast Heaven, and which adorns it after the Father, but her dominion is established on high.

20. The Soul, being a brilliant Fire by the power of the Father, remains immortal, as Mistress of Life, filling up the many recesses of the bosom of the World.

21. The channels being intermixed, she performs the works of incorruptible Fire therein.

22. For not in Matter did the Fire which is in the first beyond enclose His active Power, but in Mind; for the framer of the Fiery World is the Mind of Mind.

23. He who first sprang from Mind, clothing the one Fire with the other Fire, and binding them together, so that he might mingle the fountainous craters, while preserving unsullied the brilliance of His own Fire.

24. And thence a Fiery Whirlwind drawing is down the brilliance of the flashing flame and penetrates the abysses of the Universe; From thence downwards do extend their wondrous rays.

25. The Monad first existed, and the Paternal Monad still subsists.

26. When the Monad is extended, the Dyad is generated.

27. Beside Him is seated the Dyad glittering with intellectual sections, which govern all things and to order everything not ordered.

28. The Mind of the Father, whose Will assented, said that all things should be cut into Three, and immediately all things were so divided.

29. The Mind of the Eternal Father split into Three, governing all things by Mind.
30. The Father mingled every Spirit from this Triad.

31. All things are supplied from the bosom of this Triad.

32. All things are governed and subsist in this Triad.

33. You must know that all things bow before the Three Supernals.

34. Not that first essence, but that whereby all things are measured does flow forth the first triad; being pre-existent

35. There appeared in it Virtue and Wisdom, and multiscient Truth.

36. In each World shines the Triad, over which the Monad rules.

37. The First Course is Sacred; in the middle lace courses the Sun, and in the third the Earth is heated by the internal fire.

38. It is exalted upon High; animating Light, Fire, Ether and Worlds.

IDEAS.

INTELLIGIBLES, INELLECTUALS, IYNGES, SYNOCHES, TELETARCHAE, FOUNTAINS, PRINCIPLES, HECATE, AND DAEMONS.

39. The Mind of the Father whirled forth in reechoing roar, comprehending by invincible Will Ideas omniform; which, flying forth from that one fountain issued from the Father alike as the Will and the End; by which they are connected with the Father according to alternating life, through varying vehicles. They were divided asunder by Intellectual Fire and distributed into other Intellectuals. For the King of all previously placed before the polymorphous World is both intellectual and incorruptible. The imprint of whose form is sent forth through the World, by which the Universe shines forth decked with Ideas of all variation, of which the foundation is One; One and alone (all-one). From this the others rush forth; distributed and separated through the various bodies of the Universe, and are borne in swarms through its vast abysses; ever whirling forth in illimitable radiation. These are the intellectual conceptions from the Paternal Fountain whom partake abundantly of the brilliance of Fire in the culmination of unresting Time. However; it is the primary self-perfect Fountain of the Father that poured forth these primo genial Ideas.

40. These being many, descend flashingly upon the shining Worlds, and in them are contained the Three Supernals.

41. They are the guardians of the works of the Father, and of the One Mind, the Intelligible.

42. All things subsist together in the Intelligible World.

43. All intellect understands the deity, for intellect exists neither without the Intelligible, nor apart from Intellect does the Intelligible subsist.

44. Intellect exists not without the Intelligible; apart from it, it subsists not.

45. By Intellect He contains the Intelligibles and introduces the Soul into the Worlds.

46. By Intellect he contains the Intelligibles, and introduces Sense into the Worlds.

47. This Paternal Intellect, which comprehends the Intelligibles and adorns things ineffable, has sown symbols through the World.

48. This Order is the beginning of all section.

49. The Intelligible is the principle of all section.

50. The Intelligible is as food to that which understands.

51. The oracles concerning the Orders exhibits it as prior to the Heavens, as ineffable, and they add -- It has Mystic Silence.

52. The oracle calls the Intelligible causes Swift, and asserts that, proceeding from the Father, they rush again unto Him.
53. Those Natures are both Intellectual and Intelligible, which, themselves possessing Intellection, are the objects of Intelligence to others.

54. The Intelligible Iynges themselves understand from the Father; by Ineffable counsels being moved so as to understand.

55. It instills into the Synoches the enlivening strength of Fire endued with mighty Power; because, it is the Operator, the Giver of Life Bearing Fire, and because it fills the Life-producing bosom of Hecate.

56. He gave His own Whirlwinds to guard the Supernals, mingling the proper force of His own strength in the Synoches.

57. But likewise as many as serve the material Synoches.

58. The Teletarchs are comprehended in the Synoches.

59. Rhea, the Fountain and River of the Blessed Intellectuals, having first received the powers of all things in Her Ineffable Bosom, pours forth perpetual Generation upon all things.

60. For it is the bound of the Paternal Depth, and the Fountain of the Intellectuals.

61. For He is a Power of circumlucid strength, glittering with Intellectual Sections.

62. He glitters with Intellectual Sections and has filled all things with love.

63. Unto the Intellectual Whirlings of Intellectual Fire, all things are subservient, through the persuasive counsel of the Father.

64. How the World has inflexible Intellectual Rulers.

65. The source of the Hecate corresponds with that of the Fontal Fathers.

66. From Him leap forth the Amilicti, the all-relentless thunders; and the whirlwind receiving Bosoms of the all-splendid Strength of Hecate, Father-begotten; he who encircles the Brilliance of Fire; and the Strong Spirit of the Poles, all fiery beyond.

67. There is another Fountain, which leads the Empyraean World.

68. The Fountain of Fountains, and the boundary of all fountains.

69. Under two Minds the Life-generating fountain of Souls is comprehended.

70. Beneath them exists the Principal One of the Immaterials.

71. Father begotten Light, which alone has gathered from the strength of the Father the Flower of mind, and has the power of understanding the Paternal mind, and instils into all Fountains and Principles the power of understanding and the function of ceaseless revolution.

72. All fountains and principles whirl round and always remain in a ceaseless revolution.

73. These Principles, which have understood the Intelligible works of the Father, Have been clothed in sensible works and bodies; being intermediate links and existing to connect the Father with Matter; which renders apparent the Images of unapparent Natures, and to inscribe the Unapparent in the Apparent frame of the World.

74. Typhon, Echidna, and Python, being the progeny of Tartaros and Gaia, united by Uranos; form, as it were, a certain Chaldæan Triad; the Inspector and Guardian of all the *disordered* fabrications.

75. There are certain Irrational Demons (mindless elementals), which derive their subsistence from the Aërial Rulers; wherefore the Oracle says, Being the Charioteer of the Aërial, Terrestrial and Aquatic Dogs.

76. The Aquatic, when applied to Divine Natures, signifies a Government inseparable from Water. Hence, the Oracle calls the Aquatic Gods, "Water Walkers".

77. As Zoroaster taught, especially in Persia and Africa. There are certain Water Elementals, whom Orpheus calls Nereides;

whom dwell in the more elevated exhalations of Water, may appear in damp, cloudy Air, and whose bodies are sometimes seen by more acute eyes.

PARTICULAR SOULS.

SOUL, LIFE, AND MAN.

78. The Father conceived ideas and all mortal bodies were animated by Him.

79. For the Father of Gods and men placed the Mind in the Soul; and placed both of them in the body.

80. The Paternal Mind has sown symbols in the Soul.

81. Having mingled the Vital Spark from two according substances, Mind and Divine Spirit, as a third to these He added Holy Love, the venerable Charioteer uniting all things.

82. Thus Filling the Soul with profound Love.

83. The Soul of man does in a manner clasp God to herself. Having nothing mortal, she is wholly inebriated with God. She glories in the harmony under which the mortal body subsists.

84. The more powerful Souls perceive Truth through themselves and are of a more inventive Nature. According to the Oracle, such Souls are saved through their own strength.

85. The Oracle says that Ascending Souls sing a Pæan.

86. Of all Souls, those certainly are superlatively blessed, which are poured forth from Heaven to Earth. They are happy and have ineffable stamina; for they proceed from Your Splendid Self, O King; even as many as from Jove Himself, under the strong necessity of Mithus.

87. The Souls of those who quit the body violently are most pure.

88. The girders of the Soul, which give her breathing, are easy to be unloosed.

89. For when you see a Soul set free, the Father sends another, that the number may be complete.

90. Understanding the works of the Father, they avoid the shameless Wing of Fate and are placed in God, drawing forth strong light-bearers. Descending from the Father, from whom as they descend, the Soul gathers the empyræan fruits of the soul-nourishing flower.

91. This Animastic Spirit, which blessed men have called the Pneumatic Soul, becomes a God; an all-various Dæmon, and a disembodied Image. In this form, Soul suffers her punishments. The Oracles also accord with this account, for they assimilate the employment of the Soul in Hades to the delusive visions of a dream.

92. From widely distributed sources, one Life after another passes from above; through to the opposite art; through the Centre of the Earth; and to the fifth middle, the fiery centre, where the life-bearing fire descends as far as the material world.

93. Water is a symbol of life. Hence; Plato and the gods before Plato, sometimes call it the whole water of vivification, and yet sometimes, a certain fountain of it.

94. O Man, of daring nature, you're a subtle production!

95. The beasts of the Earth shall in habit your vessel .

96. Since the Soul perpetually runs and passes through many experiences in a certain space of time; which being performed, it is then compelled to pass back again through all things, and unfold a similar web of generation in the World. According to

Zoroaster, "as often as the same causes return, the same effects will in like manner be sure to ensue."

97. According to Zoroaster, it is inside us that the ethereal vestment of the Soul perpetually revolves.

98. The Oracles delivered by the Gods celebrate the essential fountain of every Soul; the Empyrean, the Ethereal and the Material. This fountain they separate from the vivifying Goddess. From this goddess, they make two series or orders; the one animastic; or belonging to the Soul; the other belonging to Fate. They assert that the Soul is derived from the animastic series, yet sometimes it becomes subservient to Fate; such as passing into an irrational condition of being, becoming subject to Fate instead of to Providence.

MATTER.

THE WORLD – AND NATURE.

99. The Matrix containing all things.

100. Wholly divisible; yet indivisible.

101. From thence abundantly springs forth the generations of multifarious Matter.

102. These frame atoms, sensible forms, corporeal bodies, and things destined to matter.

103. The Nymphs of the Fountains, all the Water Spirits; as well as the terrestrial, aërial and astral forms, are the Lunar Riders and Rulers of all Matter. They are the Celestial, the Starry, and that which lies in the Abysses.

104. According to the Oracles, Evil is more feeble than Non-entity.
105. We learn from the oracles that Matter pervades the whole world, as the Gods also assert.

106. All Divine Natures are incorporeal, but bodies are bound to them for your sakes. Bodies are unable to restrain incorporeals, by reason of the Corporeal Nature, in which you are concentrated.

107. The paternal Self-begotten Mind, understands His works sown in All and the fiery bonds of love; so that all things might continue loving for an infinite time. The elements of the world continue their course in mutual attraction so that the connected series of things might intellectually remain in the Light of the Father.

108. The self-operating Maker of all things, framed the World. and there was a certain Mass of Fire. All these self-Operating things He produced so that the Body of the Universe might be conformed; that the World might be manifest, and not appear membranous.

109. He assimilates the images to himself, casting them around his own form.
110. They are an imitation of his Mind, but that which is fabricated has something of a Body.

111. There is a Venerable Name with a sleepless revolution, which is leaping forth into the worlds, through the rapid tones of the Father.

112. Therefore the Ethers of the Elements are there.

113. The Oracles assert that several types of characters, and other Divine visions appear in the Ether.

114. In this the things without figure are figured.

115. The Ineffable and Effable impressions of the World.

116. The Light hating World and the winding currents by which many are drawn down.

117. He makes the whole World of Fire, Air, Water, and Earth, and of the all-nourishing Ether.
118. Placing Earth in the middle, but Water below the Earth, and Air above both these.
119. He affixed a vast multitude of un-wandering Stars, not by a strain laborious and hurtful, but with a stable void of movement; forcing Fire forward into Fire.

120. The Father congregated the Seven Firmaments of the Kosmos, thus circumscribing the Heavens with convex form.

121. He constituted a Septenary of wandering Existences (the Planetary globes).

122. He suspended their disorder in Well-disposed Zones.

123. He made six in number, and for the Seventh He cast into the midst thereof: the Fiery Sun.

124. The Centre forms from where all (lines); any which way are equal.

125. That the Swift Sun passes as ever around such a Centre.

126. Eagerly urging itself towards that Centre of resounding Light.

127. The Vast Sun and the Brilliant Moon.

128. As rays of Light his locks flow forth; ending in acute points.

129. The Solar Circles; the Lunar, clashings, and of the Aerial Recesses; the Melody of Ether, and of the Sun, and of the phases of the Moon, and of the Air.

130. The most mystic of discourses informs us, and the Oracles of the Chaldæans affirm, that His wholeness is in the Supramundane Orders; for there a Solar World and Boundless Light subsist.

131. The Sun truly measures all things by time; being itself the time of time, according to the Oracle of the Gods concerning it.
132. According to the telestic Hypothesis, the Disk (of the Sun) is borne in the Starless realm above the Inerratic Sphere; and hence he is not in the midst of the Planets; but of the Three Worlds.

133. The Sun is a Fire, the Channel of Fire, and the dispenser of Fire.

134. Hence Kronos, The Sun as Assessor beholds the true pole.

135. The Ethereal Course, and the vast motion of the Moon, and the Aerial fluxes.

136. Æther, Sun, and Spirit of the Moon, are the chiefs of the Air.

137. The wide Air, the Lunar Course, and the Pole of the Sun.

138. The Goddess brings forth the Vast Sun, and the lucent Moon.

139. As she collects it, she recieves the Melody of æther; of the Sun, the Moon, and of whatsoever which is contained in the Air.

140. Unwearied Nature rules over the Worlds and works, so that the Heavens drawing downward might run an eternal course, and so that the other periods of the Sun and Moon, (Seasons; Night and Day); might be accomplished.

141. Above the shoulders of that Great Goddess Nature is exalted in her vastness .

142. Together with Ostanes and Zoroaster, the most celebrated of the Babylonians, very properly call the starry Spheres "Herds". These alone among corporeal magnitudes are perfectly carried about around a Centre. In conformity to the Oracles, they are considered, in a certain respect, as the bonds and collectors of physical reasons; which they likewise call in their sacred discourse, "Herds"; and by the insertion of a gamma, Angels. Wherefore the Stars which preside over each of these "herds" are considered to be either Deities or Dæmons. They are similar to the Angels, and are called Archangels; and they are seven in number.

143. Zoroaster calls the congruities of material forms to the ideals of the Soul of the World, "Divine Allurements."

MAGICAL AND PHILOSOPHICAL PRECEPTS.

144. Direct not your mind to the vast surfaces of the Earth, for the Plant of Truth grows not upon the ground.; nor measure the motions of the Sun, collecting rules, for he is carded by the Eternal Will of the Father, and not for your sake alone. Dismiss the impetuous course of the Moon, for she moves always by the power of necessity. The progression of the Stars was not generated for your sake. The wide aerial flight of birds gives no true knowledge nor the dissection of the entrails of victims; they are all mere toys; the basis of mercenary fraud.. Flee from these if you would enter the sacred paradise of piety, where Virtue, Wisdom, and Equity are assembled.

145. Stoop not down unto the Darkly-Splendid World. Therein continually lies a faithless Depth; Hades wrapped in clouds; delighting in unintelligible images. Precipitous and winding; a black ever-rolling Abyss which is ever espousing a Body unluminous, formless and void.

146. Stoop not down by a descending Ladder which has Seven Steps, for a precipice lies beneath the Earth and therein is established the Throne of an evil and fatal force.

147. Stay not on the Precipice with the dross of Matter, for there is an ever-splendid place for your image.

148. Invoke not the visible Image of the Soul of Nature.

149. Look not upon Nature, for her name is fatal.

150. It does not become you to behold the divine allurements before your body is initiated, since by always alluring they seduce the souls from the sacred mysteries.

151. Bring her not forth, lest in departing she retain something.

152. Defile not the Spirit, nor deepen a superficies.

153. Enlarge not your Destiny.

154. Not hurling, according to the Oracle, a transcendent foot towards piety.

155. Change not the barbarous Names of Evocation; for there are sacred Names in every language which are given by God, having in the Sacred Rites a Power Ineffable.

156. Go not forth when the Lictor passes by.

157. May hope nourish you upon the fiery Angelic plane.

158. The conception of the glowing Fire has the first rank. The mortal who approaches that Fire shall have Light from God and unto this persevering mortal the Blessed Immortals are swift.

159. The Gods exhort us to understand the radiating form of Light.

160. It becomes you to hasten unto the Light and to the Rays of the Father; from whom a Soul imbued with much Mind was sent unto you .

161. Seek Paradise.

162. Learn the Intelligible for it subsists beyond the Mind.

163. There is a certain Intelligible One whom it becomes you to understand with the Flower of Mind.

164. The Paternal Mind accepts not the aspiration of the soul until she has passed out of her oblivious state by pronouncing the Word and regaining the Memory of the pure paternal Symbol.

165. Unto some He gives the ability to receive the Knowledge of Light. Even those who are "asleep" are made fruitful from His own strength.

166. It is not proper to understand that Intelligible One with vehemence, but with the extended flame of far reaching Mind, measuring all things except that Intelligible. It is requisite to understand this; for if you inclined your Mind you would understand it, not earnestly; but it is becoming to bring with you a pure and enquiring sense; to extend the void mind of your Soul to the Intelligible so that you may know the Intelligible, because it subsists beyond Mind.

167. You wilt not comprehend it, as when under-standing some common thing.

168. You who understand, know the Super-mundane Paternal Depth.

169. Things Divine are not attainable by mortals who understand the body alone. Only those who are stripped of their garments arrive at the summit.

170. Having put on the completely armed-vigor of resounding Light of triple strength; fortifying the Soul and the Mind, He must then put the various Symbols into the Mind. Do not walk dispersedly on the empyrean path, but with concentration.

171. For not only being furnished with every kind of Armor, but so armed, he is similar to the Goddess.

172. Whence, or which ever order you have come; explore the River of the Soul, so that although you have become a servant to the body, you may again rise to the Order from which you descended; joining works to sacred reason.

173. Every way unto the emancipated Soul extend the rays of Fire.

174. Let the immortal depth of your Soul lead you, but earnestly raise your eyes upwards.

175. Man, as an intelligent Mortal, must bridle his Soul that she may not incur terrestrial infelicity, but be saved.

176. If you extend the Fiery Mind to the work of piety, you will preserve the fluxible body.

177. The telestic life through Divine Fire removes all the stains; together with everything of a foreign and irrational nature. As we are taught by the Oracle to believe that the spirit of the Soul has attracted from generation,

178. The Oracles of the Gods declare, that through purifying ceremonies, not only the Soul , but also bodies in and of themselves become Worthy of receiving much assistance and health, for, as they say; "the mortal vestment of coarse Matter will by these means be purified." And this, the Gods, in an exhortatory manner, announce to the most holy of Theurgists.

179. According to the Oracle, we should flee the multitude of men going in a herd.

180. He who knows himself, knows all things in himself.

181. The Oracles often give victory to our own choice, instead of the Order of the Mundane periods. For instance, when they say, "On beholding yourself, fear!" They also say, "Believe yourself to be above the Body, and you are so." Further still, they assert; "That our voluntary sorrows germinate in us the growth of the particular life we lead."

182. These are mysteries which are evolved in the profound Abyss of the Mind.

183. As the Oracle there forth says: "God is never so turned away from man, and never so much as sends him new paths, when he makes ascent to divine speculations or works in a confused or disordered manner; with unhallowed lips, or unwashed feet." For of those who are thus negligent, the progress is imperfect, the impulses are vain, and the paths are dark.

184. Not knowing that every God is good, you are fruitlessly vigilant.

185. Theurgists fall, so as not to be ranked among the herd that are in subjection to Fate.

186. According to Chaldaic philosophy, as Porphyry informs us, the number nine is divine; receives its completion from three triads, and attains the summits of theology.

187. In the left side of Hecate is a fountain of Virtue, which remains entirely within her, not sending forth its virginity.

188. The earth bewailed them, even unto their children.

189. The Furies are the Constrainers of Men.

190. Lest being baptized to the Furies of the Earth, and to the necessities of nature (as some one of the Gods say), you should perish.

191. Nature persuades us that there are pure Dæmons, and that evil germs of Matter may alike become useful and good.

192. For three days and no longer need you sacrifice.

193. So therefore first the Priest who governs the works of Fire, must sprinkle with the Water of the loud-resounding Sea.

194. Labour you around the Strophalos of Hecate.

195. When you shall see a Terrestrial Dæmon approaching, Cry aloud! And sacrifice the stone Mnizourin.

196. If you invoke often, you shall see all things growing dark; and then when the High-arched Vault of Heaven is no longer visible to you and the Stars have lost their Light while the Lamp of the Moon is veiled. Here the Earth abides not, and around you darts the Lightning Flame as all things appear amid thunders.

197. The terrestrial, Dog-faced demons leap forth from the Cavities of the Earth; showing no true sign unto mortal man.

198. A similar Fire flashingly extends through the rushings of Air. A formless fire; whence comes the Image of a Voice, a flashing Light abounding and revolving; whirling forth; even crying aloud. Also, there is the vision of the fire-flashing Courser of Light, or of a Child, borne aloft on the shoulders of the Celestial Steed, fiery, or clothed with gold; naked while shooting shafts of Light with the bow; while standing on the shoulders of the horse. Then, if your meditation prolongs itself, you shall unite all these Symbols into the Form of a Lion.

199. When you behold that holy and formless Fire shining flashingly through the depths of the Universe, you will hear the Voice of Fire.

ORACLES FROM PORPHYRY.

1. There is above the Celestial Lights an Incorruptible Flame always sparkling; the Spring of Life, the Formation of all Beings, the Original of all things! This Flame produces all things, and nothing perishes but what it consumes. It makes Itself known by Itself. This Fire cannot be contained in any Place, it is without Body and without Matter. It encompasses the Heavens. And there goes out from it little Sparks, which make all the Fires of the *Sun,* of the *Moon,* and of the *Stars.* Behold! what I know of God! Strive not to know more of Him, for that is beyond your capacity, how ever wise you are. As to the rest, know that unjust and wicked Man cannot hide himself from the Presence of God! No subtlety nor excuse can disguise anything from His piercing Eyes. All is full of God, and God is in All!

2. There is in God an Immense Profundity of Flame! Nevertheless, the Heart should not fear to approach this Adorable Fire, or to be touched by it; it will never be consumed by this sweet Fire, whose mild and Tranquil Heat makes the Binding, the Harmony, and the Duration of the World. Nothing subsists but by this Fire, which is God Himself. No Person begat Him; He is without Mother; He knows all things, and can be taught nothing. He is Infallible in His designs, and His name is unspeakable, Behold now, what God is! As for us who are His messengers, We *are but a Little Part of God.*